Others Had It Worse

A Bur Oak Book

Holly Carver, series editor

Vetra Melrose Padget Covert and Chris D. Baker

OTHERS HAD IT WORSE

Sour Dock, Moonshine, & Hard Times
in Davis County, Iowa

University of Iowa Press, Iowa City

University of Iowa Press, Iowa City 52242
Copyright © 2013 by Chris D. Baker
www.uiowapress.org
Printed in the United States of America

Design by Kristina Kachele Design, llc

The University of Iowa Press is a member of Green Press Initiative
and is committed to preserving natural resources.

Printed on acid-free paper

Library of Congress Cataloging-in-Publication Data
Covert, Vetra Melrose Padget, 1916–1990.
Others had it worse: sour dock, moonshine, and hard times in Davis County, Iowa /
Vetra Melrose Padget Covert and Chris D. Baker.
pages   cm. — (A bur oak book)
Includes bibliographical references.
ISBN 978-1-60938-182-0, 1-60938-182-3 (pbk)
1. Covert, Vetra Melrose Padget, 1916–1990 — Childhood and youth.
2. Davis County (Iowa) — Rural conditions — 20th century. 3. Davis County (Iowa) —
Economic conditions — 20th century. 4. Davis County (Iowa) — Biography.
5. Rural families — Iowa — Davis County. 6. Prohibition — Iowa — Davis County.
7. Fathers and daughters — Iowa — Davis County — Biography. 8. Children of
alcoholics — Iowa — Davis County — Biography. I. Baker, Chris D., 1956–. II. Title.
F627.D2C68 2013
977.7'97033 — dc23   2013007169

For my mother, Betty Durham

Tis the song, the sigh of the weary,
Hard Times, hard times, come again no more
Many days you have lingered around my cabin door;
Oh hard times come again no more.

Stephen Foster, "Hard Times Come Again No More"

CONTENTS

Acknowledgments xi

A Family Portrait Reframed, by Chris D. Baker 3

The Log Cabin 23

Family Life 33

Getting By 49

Life on the Farm 61

Moonshine 73

Hunting 79

The Neighbors 87

Country School 95

Social Life 115

Sources 123

ACKNOWLEDGMENTS

I want to thank Leon Wilkinson, Reva Padget Wilkinson's son, and Betty Durham, my mother, for providing their stories and many of the family photographs in this book; my brother and sister, Mike Baker and Kim Wilkerson, for their ongoing support; my dear friend Melinda Simmons, for her editing contributions; longtime Iowa journalist and author Dean Gabbert, for his words of encouragement; old friends Steve Kapp and Kevin Finkel, for dispensing their medicinal wit during the course of this project and beyond; and, of course, my wife, Susan, and son, Miles, for their patience.

Others who contributed to this project include family members Donald Padget, the late Jean Padget, Sharon Ancell, Floyd Covert, Bill Covert, Sheri Guthrie, and Dennis Covert. I also want to thank Karl Downing, Carl J. Jackson, Pam Rietsch, Rudy Evans, and Bruce Piper. Finally, I want to acknowledge the folks at the University of Iowa Press for their collective editing, design, and marketing efforts—especially Holly Carver, who embraced the original manuscript and gently encouraged me to look beyond my initial vision for this book.

Others Had It Worse

This 1895 map shows the abandoned village of Chequest, Iowa, located between Bloomfield and Floris, approximately eighteen miles from the Missouri border. Courtesy of Pam Rietsch.

A FAMILY PORTRAIT REFRAMED

Chris D. Baker

Looking back, it is easy to understand how we lose sight of the past, our lineage. Childhood memories fade along with the names and faces of near and distant relatives. We push forward with our own lives until one day, perhaps some fifty years later, when asked about those ancestors, the answer we give is sadly insufficient: "Well, I don't really remember my great-grandfather. I think I met him once when I was a kid."

If we are lucky, a few tattered and creased photographs remain. At first glance, those often blurred and poorly exposed images seem incredibly ordinary. They certainly lack the artistry and technical expertise of a Dorothea Lange, who documented the desolate lives of Americans during the Great Depression for the Farm Security Administration. However, despite the perceived flaws, family snapshots are iconic in their own right. The captured faces bear the same harsh contours of old-world ethnicity, of untold hard times, of promise. If we are twice lucky, those photographs lend context to the mystery of our own lives.

Still, there is a void. Something is missing—something that even Lange could only intimate in her classic image, "Migrant Mother." Perhaps, it is our own mortality reflected in the eyes of aging parents and, in turn, our children, that makes filling that void suddenly urgent. Old family photographs are scrutinized for insight, but in essence we are looking at strangers. We need more. We need words. Stories. This book is an attempt to fill that void. It is a collection of family stories—better yet, I like to think of it as an excerpt from an ongoing folk song passed from one generation to the next, a song that would make Woody Guthrie proud. Over the years, the melody has surely been altered to reflect the mood and times. Sadly, some verses have been lost forever, so we don't really know how the song begins, let alone how it may end. We can, however, take comfort in the certainty that, like any family, it is indeed a work in progress.

Vetra Melrose Padget is the lyricist. Of course, to me, by virtue of her marriage to James Oscar Covert and the subsequent birth of my mother, Betty Arlene Covert, she is and will always be Grandma Covert.

Born January 1, 1916, she grew up in rural Davis County, Iowa, with her parents, Wilmer and Edith Padget, and seven siblings: Clell, Lale, Barbara, Reva, Paul, Charles, and Donald. The eighth and eldest sibling, Silas, died three days after his birth in 1903. They lived in a dilapidated log cabin near Chequest, a village once located northeast of Bloomfield near Troy, or, as the crow flies, about eighteen miles from the Missouri border.

There were two rooms up, two rooms down. No plumbing. No electricity. Holes in the roof. Holes in the floor. Holes so big, according to my grandmother, "you could of throwed a cat through them."

Based on references throughout the handwritten manuscript, matched with an overlay of birth dates, census reports, and the details of stories from extended family members, a timeline emerges indicating that the content covers her childhood from approximately age four to thirteen, or the years 1920 to 1929.

To better understand my grandmother's world, it is helpful to view those years in the context of historical events and her complicated, if not embittered, relationship with her father.

In contrast to the prosperity usually associated with the Roaring Twenties, farm prices were in a tailspin throughout that same decade. As a result, many American families were on the breadline long before the stock market crash of 1929, or before Lange first left the comfort of her portrait studio in the early 1930s to photograph the gathering crowds at the White

Angel Jungle, a San Francisco soup kitchen for the destitute. With the Great Depression looming, some historians estimate that eight million rural Americans were already struggling to just get by, to survive.

The Padget family is no exception. The poverty described herein is as inescapable as the often harsh behavior of my great-grandfather.

Wilmer, who answered to the nickname Beef, was a moon-shiner, a bootlegger. Although he stood six feet two inches and weighed about 225 pounds in his prime, he reportedly earned the moniker not for his imposing physical presence or his notoriety for drinking and fighting, but rather for consuming a large pot of beef intended for a den of fellow fox hunters.

Either way, the nickname is a plausible fit.

In the 1920 and 1930 federal census reports, his occupation is listed as a farmer, but he was not a typical farmer by any stretch, according to Leon Wilkinson, Reva Padget Wilkinson's son.

Chequest blacksmith shop, circa 1895. The business remained open into the 1920s. Courtesy of Rudy Evans. Don Piper Collection.

Chris D. Baker

"Grandpa measured his corn yield in gallons, not bushels," Leon said.

Indeed. Wilmer made moonshine, sold moonshine, and apparently consumed it with ferocity — often with staggering consequences for his family. The stories, taken from my grandmother's manuscript and gleaned piecemeal from family members, often read like indictments.

My grandmother recalls her father's habit of disappearing for days at a time, presumably to run his hunting dogs, and the constant presence of his drunken cronies, one whom she describes as passed out on the cabin floor and soaked in his own urine.

"When he came awake he just wore the same old clothes. Maybe he would be there several days," she writes. "The smell was strong."

To suggest that hard economic times pressed Wilmer and countless others into bootlegging as a matter of survival is certainly a noble, if not defensible assumption for some. However, it is sometimes difficult to distinguish an act of desperation from a mere rationalization. Clearly, in my grandmother's eyes, her father's reasoning fell to the latter and only increased the family's burden.

Edith Caruthers and Wilmer Padget on their wedding day, February 10, 1902.
Courtesy of Leon Wilkinson.

Christmas was a particularly confusing and sad time for the Padget children. At best, each received a pair of stockings and, perhaps, there might be one bag of candy to be shared by all. Other years, nothing.

My grandmother recounts one Christmas during which she and her younger brothers concluded that they might receive more presents, like the other kids at school, if only they had a proper Christmas tree. After cutting a tree and fashioning a paper chain for the decoration, they thought they had it made. When morning arrived, they were disappointed.

"We tho't Santa didn't like us," she writes.

My grandmother later told her daughter, Sheri Guthrie, that during the early years of her marriage, my grandfather always cut and decorated two Christmas trees in an attempt to ease those painful childhood memories, to somehow bring balance to his bride's world.

Dennis Covert, my cousin, once attempted to bring some perspective to the grinding poverty. Upon hearing similar stories as a teenager, he offered our grandmother the standard viewpoint that everybody was poor back in the day.

"Not that poor," she replied.

My great-grandmother, Edith, seemed perpetually stuck by her husband's roguish bent. By all family accounts she did not condone Wilmer's passion for drink. Still, according to Leon Wilkinson, she hid the hooch in the washing machine when a stranger or the local sheriff came knocking.

Edith's complicity is easily reframed as an act of self-preservation. After decades of failed legislation and social unrest, Iowa had finally become a dry state in 1916, the same year my grandmother was born and four years before the passage of the 18th Amendment. If convicted of moonshining the penalty was stiff. Although the punishment was often subjective based on the will of local authorities to enforce the law, an offender could be fined up to $500 or receive six months in the county jail. Multiple offenses could land a bootlegger in the state penitentiary for up to one year. Obviously, Edith did not want her husband arrested.

Wilmer's illicit activities also attracted the attention of a higher authority. Donald Padget, my grandmother's youngest and lone surviving sibling who was born in 1923, said, "Dad got wind that they were eyeing him for moonshining. Feds came and turned the house upside down but they never found anything."

My uncle, Bill Covert, explained why the federal agents came up empty-handed, "Mom said they hid the jars of booze under the fence posts around the yard."

Wilmer was also the source of Edith's estrangement from her parents, Silas and Grace Caruthers, and her brother, Albert. Apparently, Wilmer irreparably severed all family ties to the Caruthers because he thought his mother-in-law was too bossy. As the story goes, some forty years later, an aged Edith, sitting on a park bench on the town square in Bloomfield, was approached by a man.

"You don't recognize me, do you?"

Edith Padget's family, the Caruthers, circa 1900. Left to right, Silas, Albert, Grace, and Edith. Courtesy of Leon Wilkinson.

She did not.

"I'm your brother. Albert," he said.

Clell, my great-uncle, suffered from an affliction that left him somewhat of a lifelong dependent of his parents and siblings. Although respected as a hard worker, he might be politely described as a little slow. He never married, never had kids.

When interviewing relatives about Clell's condition, different accounts emerge. One version is that he contracted scarlet fever as a child, but there are also whispers that Wilmer worked his eldest surviving son so hard in the fields that, at age seven or eight, Clell suffered a heat stroke. The latter is quietly, if not reluctantly, accepted by some family elders, but not all.

"I was told he was born that way," Donald Padget said of his older brother, who was eighteen years his senior. "That's all I know."

The truth is buried with Wilmer and Edith.

Finally, my grandmother recounts one of her many sleepwalking episodes that left family members in a state of panic—all, but apparently one. During the frantic search, Wilmer announced, "Well if she is gone she's gone."

Curiously, this story is not punctuated by my grandmother's oft-used reminder to the reader of her humorous intent: "Ha.

Edith and Wilmer Padget, circa 1958. Edith passed away in 1959, Wilmer in 1971. Courtesy of Betty Durham.

Chris D. Baker

Ha." As a father, I play that scene over and over in my mind. The most forgiving interpretation of those words leaves Wilmer wanting in ways difficult to reconcile.

"I believe Mom was bitter about it," Floyd Covert said of his mother's relationship with her father.

Of course, it's easy, too damn easy, to judge my great-grandfather. I don't know the complete story, all the injustices, joys, or twists that shaped his life. My grandmother does not address the subject.

It is a fact that, Wilmer, at age ten, was forced by his father, James Arbuckle Padget, to work at the coal mines in nearby Laddsdale, Iowa. He drove the mules between the mines and the railroad line. After leaving the mines, he worked as a hired hand for area farmers.

As a result, he never attended school like his other siblings. He resented his father. He resented the fact that he could not read or write. In later years, Edith finally taught Wilmer to write his name so that he could sign his old age pension check.

Yet another story passed down through the family speaks to an intergenerational cycle of male violence common to many family histories, a violence endured by women and children until it becomes frightfully mundane.

As a young man, before he was married, my great-grandfather returned to the family farm one early morning after a night of carousing. His father James ordered him to take the team of horses to the field and work. Wilmer declined, said that he needed some sleep. In response, James allegedly grabbed a large gate hinge and struck his son in the head, knocking him to the ground.

"Now go have your mother sew you up and then get the team and go to work," my great-great-grandfather James reportedly told his bloodied son.

Wilmer complied.

No one can say that my great-grandfather had an easy go of it.

Donald Padget said that he doesn't remember many of the stories in this book. Seven years younger than my grandmother, he offers a more conciliatory view of his father, Wilmer.

"He was known to be pretty tough. You didn't argue with him. If he said it was raining and it wasn't, you didn't argue with him. He was considered a tough guy, but he liked to think that he was just fair. Others might not agree," Donald surmised, adding, "I thought he was pretty good to us boys."

There are hints that an elderly Wilmer tried to atone for his past. Dennis Covert witnessed our great-grandfather, as he prepared to leave after a visit, awkwardly attempt to hug our grandmother. She would have none of it. He asked her about the incident.

"Grandma basically told me that when Wilmer drank he didn't care about anybody else," Dennis recalled. "She didn't like drinking, said it just ruined everybody's life."

Now I better understand my grandmother's guarded response when I asked her many years ago why she had never consumed alcohol.

"I saw enough," she said.

Of course, the civil thing to do is just simply dismiss my great-grandfather as an ornery old cuss and embrace his antics as fodder for family reunions. I confess that I have certainly shared a few belly laughs with family members when regaled by the outrageous stories.

For example, Wilmer was once confronted by a law enforcement officer while fishing Chequest Creek. He searched the pockets of his overalls and finally admitted that he must have misplaced his fishing license. The suspicious officer, perhaps a bit overzealously or perhaps because he was a bit too familiar with Wilmer, loaded my great-grandfather and his fishing poles into his car with the promise of a ride to the pokey.

As Bill Covert tells the story, about a mile and a half down the road Wilmer asked the officer to stop the car. He had found his license.

"Where?"

"In my hat band."

Wilmer displayed the legal fishing license, gathered up his gear, exited the car, and casually walked toward a house in front of which the officer had unwittingly stopped the vehicle. Yes, it was Wilmer's house.

The Padget sisters in 1985. Left to right, Reva Wilkinson, Barbara Million, and Vetra Covert. Courtesy of Leon Wilkinson.

The Padget brothers, circa 1960. Left to right, Donald, Charles, Paul, Lale, and Clell. Courtesy of Sharon Ancell.

"Grandpa just wanted a ride home," Bill laughed.

Over the years, as such stories are told, retold, and no doubt embellished, the edges have been softened and Wilmer has received a reprieve of sorts. The accepted caricature of Wilmer is that of the harmless, yet crafty old timer whose adolescent-like irreverence for the law is better suited for a character living near Andy Griffith's fabled Mayberry, North Carolina.

Reality is a different matter.

Stepping back, a full accounting unveils the clinical portrait of a man whose sense of male privilege was only further fueled by alcohol and, no doubt, resentment toward his father.

Wilmer's family could no more escape his tyranny than he could a blow to the head with a gate hinge, than the nation could a collapsing economy. His choices, for better or worse, unequivocally shaped the lives of his wife, their children, and, perhaps, even future generations. This book is not about Wilmer Wilton Padget and, yet, it is. Simply put, my grandmother's story is inextricably bound to her father.

Vetra rode the family horse four miles to Troy to take her seventh-grade exams at the consolidated school. Built in 1915, the school closed in 1960. Courtesy of Leon Wilkinson.

Chris D. Baker

Should my interpretation of events be construed as a gratu-itous sucker punch or a smearing of the family's good name, please know that my intent is not to condemn my elders but rather to better understand and honor my grandmother's worldview, her truth. As such, any inclination to quiet her voice is a disservice to all, to posterity.

But those are my words, from my easy chair.

Others might not agree.

Although there is no apparent effort to avoid unseemly or potentially embarrassing family stories, be warned that my grandmother's candid memories are not to be confused with grievances. That was not her nature. Like so many other people of her ilk, she would have publicly shrugged off such judgments: *That's just the way it was. Others had it worse. We got by.*

Of course, there were good times and good humor to boot. She writes of her joy in attending the Toby and Susie Tent Show during the annual Fox Chase near Floris, performing the "shod-ish" at country dances, and proudly riding the family horse four miles to Troy to take her seventh-grade exams. She passed.

And it's still hard not to grin, just a little, when reading of the family cow, Spot, who inadvertently ate the mash intended for my great-grandfather's moonshine, or my grandmother's ongoing consternation with a neighbor girl left in her charge on several occasions—one Irene Humphrey.

Irene, by my grandmother's account, was as unruly as a cowlick on Sunday morning. Despite several warnings, one day Irene managed to walk through every mud puddle to be found on the way to school. Unable to remove the water-filled boots, my grandmother finally picked up the crying child and turned her upside down. Problem solved.

Other problems required more drastic measures. When illness or injury struck, Edith turned to folk remedies to meet most of the family's medicinal needs. To break up a cold, three drops of kerosene were added to a teaspoon of sugar and consumed. Kerosene, mixed with melted lard, was used to grease a chest cold. If a milk and flour poultice proved ineffective, then cow manure served as an astringent to treat a minor wound.

Donald Padget recalled another cure for a stubborn cold that my grandmother failed to mention. One-half tablespoon of skunk oil, or more accurately stated the skimmed froth from boiled skunk fat, mixed with one-fourth tablespoon of kerosene would presumably purge the body of any lingering toxins.

"You would vomit as soon as it hit your stomach," Donald said.

In assimilating the events of my grandmother's childhood, my perception of her has obviously changed. Just as it is nearly impossible for any child to embrace the notion of his own parents as once relevant or even hip, I could have never imagined my grandmother as the playful, whimsical, and sometimes ornery character portrayed in her manuscript. It's good to know that she existed.

There is also a newfound respect for my family's ability to survive despite the devastating forces at play, whether imposed or self-inflicted. It wasn't always pretty. Surely, there were regrets and, certainly, there are scars. In the end, each generation plays the hand dealt and strives to improve the lot of the next—truly, a work in progress.

As am I.

Approximately four years after the period covered in this

Donald Padget, circa 1930. Courtesy of Sheri Guthrie.

Chris D. Baker

book, my grandparents married on November 6, 1933, in Ottumwa. She was 17, he 20. They had eight kids: Floyd, my mother Betty, Beatrice, the twins William and Robert, Jerry, and late arrivals Sheri and Vicki.

After living in several rural locations in and around Davis and Wapello Counties, they eventually moved to Ottumwa proper around 1964. Their home, an old two and one-half story farmhouse with a wraparound porch, sat on a small acreage that included a small outbuilding and a barn. Part of the house was rented to a rarely seen or heard elderly woman, Mrs. Gasser, who apparently came with the house.

There, my grandmother could still tend to her chickens and her milk cow, Bossy. Each morning she emptied the milk bucket into a hand-cranked separator to strain the cream. I still cringe when I think of my grandfather drinking warm chunks of cream straight from a glass. As a city kid, I preferred store-bought milk.

By this time, my grandfather, Oscar, after working several manufacturing jobs, had settled in to what would be an eighteen-year career at Lowenberg Bakery in Ottumwa. He was a millwright. He kept the mixers, ovens, and wrapping machines running six days a week.

On Saturday afternoons, he could always be found in his threadbare overstuffed chair where he perfected the ability to remain immersed in a detective novel while simultaneously watching the St. Louis Cardinals on the television. He seemed oblivious to the chaos brought by grandchildren running amok in and out of the house, the constant slapping of wooden screen doors. Oblivious, that is, until an unsuspecting grandchild paused one second too long in the middle of the living room.

"You're in my light," he would bark, without looking up from his book.

It wasn't much of a bark.

My grandfather loved to bowl. In 1965, he and his brother-in-law Ralph White won the Ottumwa City Tournament doubles championship. They rolled a 1285. The trophy sits on a shelf in my closet.

On league night, my grandfather would occasionally load the car with kids and head toward the bowling alley. Like any serious bowler, his approach was ritualistic. Standing straight and rigid with his heels locked on the back edge of the lane, he centered the sixteen-pound ball high on his chest, took a deep breath, paused, practiced two or three backswings, paused again, and then advanced toward the pins. He threw the ball hard.

For me, his backswing was the key. As the ball reached its high point and began its downward trajectory, it would brush against his baggy pants and jingle the loose change in his pocket. I knew I had my grandfather dead to rights should he deny that he had extra money for candy and pop.

My grandmother was a homebody. When she did venture outside the house to an occasional rummage sale or auction, she truly seemed out of her element. As far back as I can remember, my grandfather did all the grocery shopping.

I cannot speak for my siblings, cousins, or extended family members, but as a child, I found my grandmother to be intimidating. Tall. White hair. Plain cotton dress. No complaints. No nonsense. Quiet.

Despite the sometimes unnerving silence, I do remember her words to me when, at about age eight or nine, I burst into her cluttered kitchen and declared that I knew a secret.

"Don't you want to know?" I teased.

"It's not a secret if you tell someone," she replied, without looking up from the pot she was stirring.

Dang. I just wanted to spill the beans; I did not ask for a lesson in personal ethics.

For all I knew, she lived in that kitchen. On just about any day, but especially the weekends, she stood between the stove and the kitchen table alternately rolling and cutting noodles, stirring soup beans, peeling and mashing potatoes, thinning gravy, kneading dough—all amid an occasional dusting of white flour. Her cinnamon rolls were to die for. Aunts, uncles, cousins, and many people I did not know feasted in that kitchen all weekend long.

On weekdays, sometime around noon I recall, she sat at that kitchen table and listened to her favorite radio show, *The Trading Post*, on 1240 KBIZ. Locals called in to buy, sell, or barter wares ranging from tillers in various stages of disrepair to canning jars, fresh eggs, and, of course, coupons and trading stamps.

My grandmother loved coupons and trading stamps: saved them, traded them, redeemed them. One Christmas, she gave some of the older grandchildren oversized Italian sunglasses that folded to the size of a single lens and fit into a nifty simulated-leather pouch. I have no idea how many books of stamps she had to save for those shades, but I remain confident that somehow, somewhere, they were once considered chic—just not in Ottumwa, Iowa, in the late 1960s.

When my grandfather died on the job of a heart attack on October 10, 1969, my grandmother seemed lost. I believe she was. Everything changed. She and the two youngest girls, Sheri and Vicki, eventually moved to a smaller house. She abandoned the kitchen for a rocking chair. She watched her stories. She took up smoking. She endured.

Blessed with the wisdom of a petulant teenager, I began to view her as hopelessly out of touch. *For crying out loud, she doesn't even know how to drive a car.* Over the next few years, I drifted away.

In 1977, as a journalism student at the University of Iowa, I received an assignment to interview a family member. I chose my grandmother and made the winding drive back to Ottumwa. Sitting on her front porch steps following the interview, I tore out the pages upon which I had scrawled my notes and handed her a yellow ruled notebook.

"Here, Grandma. You should write more about your childhood."

The last time I saw her she lived in a nursing home. I was thirty-three. She smiled as I peered around the half-opened door. I hid my shock and moved toward the only other chair. Pale and bony from the ravages of diabetes and dementia, she sat in an institutional-grade recliner, shoulders forward, back bowed, fingers curled over the tips of the armrests, elbows locked to the ready.

"Going somewhere?" I asked.

"Like to, but I reckon not," she said. "Where you been, Dad?"

I didn't hear much after that. I did not remind my grandmother that her husband, my grandfather, had long passed. I listened politely for a few minutes, pacing myself, nodding, smiling, waiting for the inevitable silence. On cue, I stood up, kissed her forehead, and turned to leave, knowing that, right or wrong, I would not return.

"Come back," she called out.

"I will."

She died a few months later on March 25, 1990.

She was seventy-four.

Some ten years later, I came across that tattered yellow notebook while rummaging through some forgotten box. Oddly, I don't remember when or how the notebook found its way back to me, but I am thankful. In perusing the pages, I immediately recognized the rhythm of the prose. I could almost hear my grandmother's voice. I closed the notebook and vowed to shape the manuscript into a gift for my mother. Of course, I promptly returned the notebook to the box and forgot about it.

Until now.

Page 1

Things I remember as a Kid growing up.

The first I can remember as a Kid was living in this log Cabin 4 rooms 2 up + 2 down. The floors had holes in it you could of throwd a cat through them. + up stairs where I slept with Barbara + Reva when it snowed on the bed we shook the snow off the covers when we got up. But luck was with us We Kids never seemed to be Very sick.

This log Cabin house was on 80 acres that they took the money from mom money she got from the estate from her folks when they died they died when Reva was a baby. This farm was mostly Covered by brush + I mean brush. Every yr Chel + Dad sometimes cut the brush + It was our Kids job to drag it to the ditch or pile it so they could burn it. (Charles/Chuck) was born in this Cabin. I remember they sent us kids down to Mart + Rasie Barkers to stay. It sure was a supprise to find a baby when we got home. Rasy wasn't very well + I wasn't very old but I would go down + stay with Rasy while mart worked in the field. If she got sick I was to go + Ring the dinner bell + he would come in a hurry. But I never had to ring it. thank goodness. They were real nice to us Kids. I had been staying with her

In preparing this work for publication, I managed to collect a handful of photographs and documents from family members and private individuals with ties to Davis County. Although not all adhere to the stated timeline, I am hopeful that, at minimum, the images convey to the reader a sense of time and place, a way of life.

The first page of Vetra's journal.

The twenty-nine-page handwritten manuscript is reproduced in its entirety save a few redundant passages. There are no footnotes related to my grandmother's writing, which may present a challenge to readers unfamiliar with rural slang. For example, when explaining the process of milling sugar cane, she writes of removing the "Rummies," extraneous bits of stalks or weeds that could spoil the molasses. In describing the family's "polivo or Fistulo" plow horses, she is likely referencing the terms poll-evil and fistula withers. Horses with those afflictions suffer from infected sores on or near the poll (neck) or withers (shoulder) where the collar rests. A curious nickname, Dobbin, also appears in the text in reference to George Pherigo, the old bachelor who lived across the road from Oak Hill School. Dobbin is an antiquated slang term for a workhorse.

In addition, I made no effort to correct misspellings, grammatical errors, or questionable syntax unless absolutely necessary to ensure clarity. I added required punctuation and capitalization to delineate obvious sentences and substituted "and" for my grandmother's use of the ampersand. In a few cases, I inserted a word that she had clearly overlooked. Finally, I organized the content by topic and added section and chapter titles for the sake of continuity and readability. To do more would be to deny a heartfelt song about Wilmer, Edith, Clell, Lale, Barbara, Reva, Vetra, Paul, Charles, and Donald—the Padget family, my family, who once lived in a log cabin out by Chequest.

So, grab 'em up and tune 'em up.

Key of G.

Are you ready?

The Log Cabin

◀ Vetra and brothers, circa 1926. Left to right, Chuck, Paul, and Don with their pet pigs in front of the log cabin. Courtesy of Floyd Covert.

TWO UP, TWO DOWN

The first I can remember as a kid was living in this log cabin 4 rooms 2 up and 2 down. The floors had holes in it. You could of throwed a cat through them. And upstairs where I slept with Barbara and Reva when it snowed on the bed we shook the snow off the covers when we got up. But luck was with us. We kids never seemed to be very sick.

LOG BY LOG

Dad bought a log house over by Chequest from Pud
Jones tore it down and built this log house we lived in
log by log. Lale and Clell cut down trees so he would
have a place to build it.

EIGHTY ACRES OF BRUSH

This log cabin house was on 80 acres. They took the money from mom. Money she got from the estate from her folks when they died. They died when Reva was a baby. This farm was mostly covered by brush and I mean brush. Every yr Clell and Dad sometimes cut the brush and it was our kids job to drag it to the ditch or pile it so they could burn it.

A BABY

(Chuck Charles) was born in this cabin. I remember they sent us kids down to Mort and Rosie Barkers to stay. It sure was a supprise to find a baby when we got home.

THE WHITE HOUSE

We lived there for a while then we moved about 1 or 2 miles maybe not that far to a nice 4 room house on a farm. We called it the white house. That is where I started to school. We lived there 3 yrs. I remember I started to school. 5 of us kids. We had a carriage with out the top and we drove the horses to it. Clell drove he was the oldest. Well we had quite a time. Not to many kids but Nora Rogers was the teacher all 3 yrs.

AUNT EFFIE

While we lived there Donald was born one night.
We were so supprised. The next morning Aunt Effie
came down and took over while mom was in bed. Boy
was she bossy. We marked the line I tell you. Don't
remember too much about those 3 yrs but going to
School.

PAUL'S BRIGHT IDEA

When we lived in the White House we had an old house for storage. Well Paul had this bright Idea he would climb up on the top of the old house and use the chimney as a toilet. I don't remember whether Dad or mom caught him or not but he finally stopped that. Ha. Ha.

BACK TO THE LOG CABIN

We moved back to the Log Cabin. A house full. I still can remember that very well. We walked to School there. If it was real real bad Clell would take us but not often.

◀ Edith Padget, Vetra's mother, circa 1940. Courtesy of Leon Wilkinson.

DON'T SASS

One time chuck done something and mom was giving him a whipping for it. Short (Paul) didn't like it so he called mom a name which was the wrong thing to do. Ha. Ha.

SMOKING

Paul was smoking and it made him sick. Mom found him laying on the bed with his head in the window to get a breeze. He asked her if that wind would help him. I think he wanted it too. He was sick.

JESUS LOVES ME

Mom told me when I was real small and young I would climb up and set on the dresser and watch myself and sing "Jesus loves me."

WHY I DID IT I NEVER KNEW

This is one on myself. Why I did it I never knew.
We kids were down at Dan Moughlers. We were all
setting in the yard. Dobin (George Pherigo) was there.
They went in to eat Dinner. We just ate before we
went down. While they were eating we set in the yard.
I was chewing gum. I took my gum and stuck it in the
bottom of one chair. Dobbin set down in that chair,
when he got up the gum strung out and Dan said
whoa there Dobbin you got gum on your pants. He
took his pocket knife and scraped it off. First one then
the other would say I wonder how that gum got on
the chair. They knew but they didn't do anything
too us.

SLEEPWALKING

I always walked in my sleep. Not because I wanted too
I just couldn't help it. I never got hurt but I would get
up in my sleep and walk around the stairway. It was
an open one and no railing. Reva decided she would
sleep in front. If I got out of bed she would catch me.
But one nite I got out of bed in the winter and took
all the covers off her and made it to the stairway
before she caught me. One nite I was just stepping off
the bottom step when I woke up. Boy I made a fast
trip back to bed. I wouldn't be down there because
everyone was sleeping up stairs.

IF SHE IS GONE, SHE'S GONE

One nite time we had company. We kids lay on the floor and went to sleep. When the company was gone Mom and Barbara was getting us to bed I was missing. Boy I guess everyone was going crazy looking and hollowring for me. Dad said well if she is gone she's gone. But finally some one found me curled up in a tire flower bed asleep. I wouldn't have been there for nothing I tell you.

TINE IN THE NECK

Charles was small and Clell was cleaning out the barn.
Charles climbed up on the wagon as Clell threw a
fork full on the wagon and stuck Charles in the neck
with one tine of the fork. Just scared Clell, Mom and of
course us kids was too. Clell brought him to the house
and Mom sent Barbara to get some flour to stop the
bleeding but no flour and hardly a spoon of Sugar. Clell
took Mom and Chuck to Troy to Dr. Garrett. He got
along fine.

HOME REMEDIES

Mom always used a poltice on sores that needed it.
If bread and milk poltice didn't work guess what
cow manure poltice. I tell you it worked. When She
greased us for a cold it was Kerosene and lard warmed
together till warm and rub it on. It worked and put
3 drops on a tsp of sugar and swallow it to break a
cold up.

CHUCK'S DOGS

Chuck liked dogs. He would make a harness for them hitch them to a scoop shovel and lead them all over. Some times the other boys would help him.

DOWN COMES THE DRESSER

Chuck liked cats too. He had a alley cat he tho't so much of. But the darn thing would go to moms dirty clothes and do its job. She didn't like that so one day she caught the cat and rubbed its nose in it which made the cat and Chuck awfully mad. He got behind the dresser and tried to push it over and kept yelling "Down comes the dresser." We thot it was funny and if something didn't please us we would holler "Down comes the dresser."

ABOUT CUT HIS BIG TOE OFF

We had a wheel of a wheelbarrow with a handle on
each side. The kids would run it around calling it their
car. Short was spinning his feet for wheels and he cut
his foot on some glass. He just about cut his big toe off.

JOYRIDE

We had this cane and we kids had it wore slick where
we slid down it in the scoop shovel. We had fun tho. Or
thot we did.

LALE'S STORY

When Lale was about 12 or so he went to work on
a farm near Floris. He worked there till he was old
enough to work else where. He went to John Morrells
plant. He stayed there quite a while then went up
around Woolson Ia to work. He met Bertha Hedges
and finally married. They had a large family her folks
did. We all went up there and stayed over one nite.
What a trip. Never so far away from home before. John
Scott and niece Kate Million had a big truck they put a
couple of boards across to make seats. Clifford Million
Kate's brother went too. Riding that far was a treat.
I used to go and stay a few days at a time with Kate.
They were in for selling moonshine too.

A SMALL GOLD MINE

The first car Lale got was a Model T Coupe. It sure
looked like a small gold mine. Dad had a Model T
touring car. It was full when we all got in it but it
wasn't often we all went at the same time.

Getting By

◀ Lilly "Irene" Humphrey, right, with her sister, Ruth, circa 1925. Irene often accompanied Vetra on her searches for wild greens. Courtesy of Carl J. Jackson.

LUGGING WATER

We had to get water from Humphrey's well down at
the bottom of a big hill lug that water up that steep
hill. Dad let Clell take the horses and hitch to a sled
and put a barrell on it and get a barrell but if we
wanted a cool drink grab the bucket and go to the
well. Seemed like some one drank a lot of water.
We got water hauled from the pond for washing
and odds and ends.

FORAGING

In the summer there was Gooseberry and Blackberrys
to be picked, then the job of stemming the Gooseber-
rys. Of course Mom and the older ones helped with
that. I never liked that job too much. It took too long.
We looked for wild strawberrys too to snack on. They
were real good too. We gathered wild onions to when
in season.

WILD GREENS

We ate a lot of wildgreens. We would go out and get 1 or 2 buckets for dinner and mom would cook them and some times (a lot) we would go back in the afternoon and get more for supper. They seemed to be good. We picked Carpenter square, dandelions, something looked like a thistle but wasn't sticky, lamb quarters, etc. Sourdock, and others.

IRENE HUMPHREY

Well Humphreys only ate greens for supper so they ask if Irene could go along and us help her get some for them. We went down toward the creek (Chesquet Creek). She would taste everything. It didn't matter what. We would tell her it was poison but that didn't matter to her. She aggravated us half to pieces I tell you. That was a job all summer long.

MAKING TRACKS

That place was good for a lot of snakes too. I was going
along singing and picking wild onions and calling the
cows. I straitened up and there was 2 big Blue Racers
all coiled and their heads was about 1 1/2 or 2 feet up
in the air coming right at me. Boy did I make tracks for
the house. Some one else went and got them. I am still
scared of snakes I tell you.

CANE PATCH

We always had a cane patch and when it was time we had to strip it. We small ones was too small to cut it but we went along when they let us. But when it was ready to put it through the mill we some times helped to throw the Rummies out of the way and if the horses didn't want to turn the mill we had to see that it kept on the move. Walk along or some time we would ride around and around. That got pretty old. But when they got it boiled down we got to get some one to make us a wooden Paddle and lick the pan. Was that good!

MAKING MOLASSES

Dad watched the pan but the boys had to keep plenty of wood there close and feed the furnace. We had a lot of molasses for the winter. And they sold some. Mom made home made bread then we ate molasses with it and pancakes too. Most everything we could we used molasses for sweetner.

RARE TREAT

Mom always made home made bread. It was always good if we could have some warm but not often.

OFF TO CHEQUEST

We had to save the cream to sell so we didn't have any butter. But mom made cottage cheese. It was good. Oh when mom needed groceries hitch up the wagon and go to "Chequest." Not a very large place at the time about two stores Blacksmith Church and school and about 2 or 3 houses and oh yes a Produce house where you could sell cream, eggs and poultry. It was a treat tho for us kids. Mom didn't go much. Just sent the older kids.

Life on the Farm

◀ When the threshing machine arrived, neighbors joined forces to complete the work. This photograph from August of 1917 includes Wilmer Padget, who is among the group standing on the separator. Other names listed on the back of the photograph include Clarence Jones, Rob Downing, Charley McNuff, Ira and Lester Prevo, Orval Earnest, ——— Earnest, G. P. Moughler, Charlie Warner, Ross Ritz, ——— Russell, Willie Birchmier, Jess Barker, Verden Moughler, Cassie Moughler, Julia Prevo, Pearl Moughler, Orlean Downing, Vergie Downing, ——— Moughler, Kenneth Downing, ——eola Moughler, Allee H———eet, Elsie Christy, and Reva Birchmier. Courtesy of Karl Downing.

SNAKE IN THE HEN HOUSE

We had several hens for us and one time we kept
finding eggs sucked in the nest. Couldn't find out
what was doing it. Finally Mom found a snake. It had
swallowed a hole egg and crawled through a hole and
there swallowed another and there he was. She sure
made fast work of him.

WE FINALLY CAUGHT HIM

We finally got a few cows. When we drove them thro the hog lot we had a pig that would suck one cow dry. We didn't know what was doing it till we finally caught him sitting up sucking away.

NO BULL, CHUCK

Chuck was small. He was down in the field digging up some cane that had come up. Roy Vaughns bull and Elmer Humphreys bull was in the pastures. They was fighting. Us kids was yelling for Chuck to come on they were fighting. Of course he didn't pay any attention till finally it soaked in what we were saying. I tell you shovel and bucket flying and so did Chuck. He came right to the house. Barbara told me this.

THREE PET PIGS

Mr. Crandell lives on the Starks place. One day he called and said he had a sow that had pigs and he wanted to sell her. If we kids would come over he would give us some pets. Well Paul, Charles and Donald and I went over. We cut across for a shorter route. Crossed the creek at a very low place and through the field. When we got there this sow just had pigs. He put all 3 in a gunny sack and we took them home. We raised them with Moms help till they was big enough to sell but Dad took the money. We didn't feel to good about that but we did have fun playing with them while they were growing up. I have a picture of the boys and the Pigs and Myself.

THE WALKING PLOW

Dad made us kids ride the tongue of a walking plow (cultivator) and drive the horses. I drove for Clell and we usually had a polivo or Fistulo horse and we always drove them and the blind ones too. Boy it was rough riding when we plowed the new ground because he wouldn't let us go around the stumps. We had to drive over them. Some times Clell would feel a little ornery and lift up the side of the plough and we would almost tip over on the hill side.

LEGS WORE OFF

When dad planted corn with a 2 row planter drawn by 2 horses he always checked it so the corn could be plowed the long and then cross plow a wk or 2 later. We kids had to follow the planter and cover the corn that wasn't planted. If we didn't the birds would eat it. We must keep up with him and I do believe that he made the horses trot. Not much fun. By evening after all day of this your legs was wore off. We didn't have much time for play it seemed to us. If they wasn't working the horses we could ride them some times.

MAKING HAY

Dad put up hay on John Sharps place on the shares. We put our hay in the barn till it was full then stacked the rest. It was us younger kids job to stomp the hay while Clell either threw it in the loft or one of the girls would throw it back so we could stomp it down. Or one of the girls would throw it back while Clell threw it in the barn but it sure was a hot job in the loft.

THE BIG THRESHING MACHINE

They cut oats with a binder. Then we had to shock the Oats. Clell was always with us. We helped him carry the bundles and some times us smaller ones could help put the shocks together. We had'nt quite learned the trick. But the day they thrashed them it was quite a thrill. The big threshing machine came and set up. Several men would come with wagons to haul the oats to the thresher and about 2 wagons would come with wagon beds on to haul the grain to the oat bin.

DAY'S END

A big dinner was cooked. Of course kids didn't eat till
after everyone else had eaten. That was the custom
then. Of course we had a big stack of straw. It sure was
fun playing on that stack of straw.

too riding that few was a treat. I used to go & stay a few days at a time with Kate. They were in for selling moonshine too.

Dad made moonshine for several years would set its in the barrell in the brush when it was time Dad would cook it off. You could smell it a mile away. Rosy & Mart knew he was doing it but never said anything on account of us kid & know they just lived on the next hill South & when they went to the cow lot they could see right over there.

I went to get our cow Spot one nite we only had one cow & she wore a bell around her neck so we could

◀ An excerpt from Vetra's original manuscript in which she writes about her father's moonshining activities.

BARREL IN THE BRUSH

Dad made moonshine for several years. Would set it in the barrell in the brush. When it was time Dad would cook it off. You could smell it a mile away. Rosy and Mort knew he was doing it but never said anything on account of us kids I know. They just lived on the next hill South and when they went to the cow lot they could see right over there.

SEE SPOT DRUNK

I went to get our cow Spot one nite. We only had one cow and she wore a bell around her neck so we could find her. I was going along singing and calling her. Finally, I thot I heard her bell and walked down that way and saw her standing sprattled legged with the bell hanging on over one ear. I went down and hit her on the rump to start her to the barn. She staggered and run her head in the ground and bawled. It scared me. I run to the house to get mom. She came back with me. She looked at her and said she was drunk. She found the barrell of mash was half gone. Spot was sure drunk. We finally got her to the barn. Her milk wasn't good for a while. But when she had her calf it was a nice big one but it couldn't get up or stand up for a long time. Barbara done the milking. She would have to hold the calf up while it sucked the cow.

SWAM LIKE A FISH

One time Dad sent Paul, Charles and Donald out to pour a jug of whiskey from a 5 gal jug. He had it hid in a corn shock. They lay down and let some run in their mouth. Chuck and Don got a little boozed up. They wanted to go swimming. Clell went with them. They couldn't much but that day They swam like a fish.

DRANK LIKE A FISH

There was always old drunken fox hunters that was laying around there. There was George Cruickshank. He drank like a fish. He would lay around on the floor or any place and pass out. He would wet all over him self from neck down. When he came awake he just wore the same old clothes. Maybe he would be there several days. The smell was strong.

Hunting

DOGFIGHT

Me and the boys took the dog out rabbit hunting a lot and this one time we went hunting with our old dog and Rowdy and a old female bird dog some of Dads friends had left there for dad to keep. We treed something in a bank. We were helping the dogs to get it and the dogs got into a fight. We tried everything to get them to stop but they would not stop. We finally had to choke them to stop them. What a day.

SWELLED HEAD

The dogs treed something in the bank across the road
from the log cabin. Of course the boys help the dogs
dig and finally got the rabbit but Paul got the worst
of it. The bushes was poisoned Oak and did his head
swell up like a large balloon. It was quite a while
before he got rid of it too. But he was sure sick too.
I don't remember any of the rest getting it.

OL' ROWDY

For some reason Dad sold old Rowdy and the man took him to Mo. Rowdy was a hound dog. You know that dog got loose drug that heavy long chain and came home. We were so happy but He got word to the man and he came and got him. We were a sorry bunch of kids.

FOX HUNTING

Dad was always away fox hunting. Some times he went and didn't come home for a wk. None of the family knew where he was at (of course the hunting was at nite with the dog.)

STAYED ALL WEEK

They had a Fox Hunt north of Floris. People put up a tent and stayed all wk if they wanted to. The family done this for several yrs. How Mom ever put up with this I don't know. Dad took his hounds and the men some of theirs and go out to listen to the dogs chase a fox. Of course each guy could tell his dog bark or so they said.

THE LAST TIME

I remember one yr School started a little early so they
never sent us to School till after the week at the Fox
Hunt. But some one turned us in and they made the
folks send us there. We never stayed that year all wk
and that was the last time all the family camped.
Mom cooked the meals on a camp fire. We had to
gather the sticks.

The Neighbors

◀ Left to right, neighbors Clarence "Pud" Jones and his wife, Grace, with Edith, Clell, and Wilmer Padget, circa 1930. Courtesy of Leon Wilkinson.

DAN AND MRS. MOUGHLER

Dan and Mrs. Moughler lived just over the hill from us and we would go there and talk to them. I wasn't very old before I started to school and she always had cookies or pie and give us some before we went home. We were there this time and she hadn't given us anything yet and I said Ho Hum I wish I had a piece of Pie. She said she was sorry but she didn't have anything that time. The kids never let me forget it.

ROY VAUGHN

I remember I would go over to Roy Vaughn's and get baby Pidgeons to bring home and put them on top of the hen house in boxes and dig fish worms for them. Some I had to hold their mouths open while I would feed them but they were pets. I could holler for them and they would fly down on my Shoulder or head. Some drunk said he would give me a dollar for one. I took the dollar but before I caught the bird I give the dollar back. I could not sell my Pidgeon.

PUD AND GRACE JONES

I took sticks and lay them on the ground and mark out my play house. I couldn't keep the pet lambs out. They wouldn't come in the door even. I got so mad I picked it up and threw him out. Of course It broke one leg. My good luck Pud Jones was there. He took some pieces of thin board made a splint and fixed its leg and he got allright.

ROSY AND MORT BARKER

Rosy wasn't very well and I wasn't very old but
I would go down and stay with Rosy while Mort
worked in the field. If she got sick I was to go and Ring
the dinner bell and he would come in a hurry. But I
never had to ring it. Thank goodness. They were real
nice to us kids. I had been staying with her. They were
going to town (Troy) to take Cream and Eggs and They
took me with them. What a Thrill going to town and
after dark too.

ELMER AND EULA HUMPHREY

Humphreys finally got a Radio. That was the first we ever heard. They would tell us kids come and listen to it. We would go at nite. Clell would go too. He would enjoy it too. We listened to Nashville and to boxing matches. It was a thrill. We all would set around the radio like we do T. V. now.

THE MILLERS

Dean and Addie and Franklin Miller was over to our place. The boys and Franklin took the dogs on a chain to the pond to get a drink. Went out on the plank. Some how Paul and Rowdy dog fell off in the pond. Paul hung on to the chain and Rowdy swam across the pond and pulled Paul out. That was something.

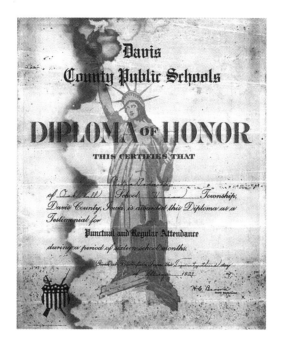

◀ In 1927, Vetra received a diploma of honor for attendance and punctuality over a sixteen-month period while attending Oak Hill School. Courtesy of Betty Durham.

DISCIPLINE

Leota Bales was our teacher. She was Paul's first
Teacher. Leland Stockdall set in the seat right behind
Paul. He was a lot older than Paul but he done
everything to get his attention to turn around. He
was showing Paul how to crack his knuckles. Leota
walked back there and asked him what he was
doing. He put his hands on the back of Pauls desk
and she whacked him one with this pencil and
brok it. This pencil was about 12 or 14 inches long
and as big around as a grown persons thumb.

A TEACHER'S GIFT

Leota Bales our teacher one yr gave me a Cupie doll
and I cried because that was the first real doll I ever
had. I kept that doll for several yrs after I was married.
I loved that doll.

PURR

One teacher we had tried to teach Charles to say poor. All he would say was purr. We heard that over and over for days. I guess he can say it now. Ha. Ha.

MINDING THE HORSES

Clell took corn and sometimes a little hay for the horses at noon. He would unhitch them and tie them to a post till we got ready for school.

THE OLD BACHELOR

Just across the road from the School an old Batchlor lived. His name was George Pherigo but everyone called him Dobin. He used to bake a cake or biscuits and bring them over to the School kids for dinner. He was sure good to all us kids at School. He was good to everyone. When the apples was ready to eat or the peaches he would bring some over for all kids. We always carried the water for School from his well. Down over the hill east. No water in the well at the School.

IRENE . . . AGAIN

We kids went over to Elmer and Eula Humphrey alot.
They had 1 girl ready to go to School. So she walked to
school with us kids. We had to take care of her. Was she
slow. I do believe that we could crawl faster than she
could walk. She walked through every mud puddle she
could find. She (Irene was her name) walked through
a water puddle and it was up over her overshoes. They
was full of water and she was crying. I couldn't get
the water out of the boots. Finally I picked her up side
down and drained the water out of them. Ha. Ha.

LIKE A FREIGHT TRAIN WOULD A BUM

Dan and Doak Moughler lives first house south of us.
They drove a model "T" 2 seater but they never ask
us kids to ride till one evening we was coming home
from School. They passed us like a freight train would
a bum. Well down on the creek bottom we called it
there was a mud hole clear across the road and quite
wide. When we got there they were stuck but we were
still out of sorts that they never offered to pick us up.
Well when we got down to the mud hole Dan said if
you kids push us out you can ride the rest of the way
to our house which was about 2 or 3 city blocks from
their place. We just waded through the mud and said
"no" it wouldn't do any good. Well we just went on. I
guess they got out some how. They wasn't there the
next morning when we went to School. Ha. Ha.

ONE DRESS

We girls had one dress most of the time to wear to
School all Winter. Some one would give Mom some
things and Mom and Barbara would make it over for
the rest. The small boys would get made over too.

HIGH-TOP SHOES

I had to wear a pr of high top shoes one Winter. Oh how I didn't want too but some one gave them to us. They came nearer fitting me than anyone so I wore them. No one else wore them at School.

EMBARRASSED

One time my black socks they came up over your
knees wore out. Just one and it had so many patches
on it. It wasn't to fix any more. So Mom found a black
sock with blue stars in some things that was given to
her and that is what I wore. I was so embarassed at
School I would go right to my seat and sit on that leg
under me. I don't know how long I wore them a plain
black stocking and one black stocking with blue stars.
But too long for me.

CHRISTMAS CAROLS

One time I panamide (act out) a song. The teacher
made me a white robe and the song was Silent Night.
There was another song but I can't think of it now.
While some of the kids sang this song I would act it
out. We would have a Christmas program too and a
tree. We sang Christmas Carols. We drew names to
exchange gifts. We usually got handkerchiefs but that
is all we could afford to give.

CHRISTMAS DAY

The other kids always got a lot of gifts that Santa Claus
brought. We got a pr of stockings. One time Mom sold
her geese she raised and got us new sock caps in our
sock. One bag of candy for all. We couldnt understand
why all the kids got so much under their tree. One yr
we kids cut a small tree and put it up. Decorated it
with chains of paper we cut and pasted together. We
thot we had it made but we never got a bit more. We
tho't Santa didn't like us.

PIE AUCTION

We had pie Suppers and programs along about
Halloween time. The girls at School and any girl that
wanted too would decorate a box with a pie in it.
Then they would auction off the pie. The teachers pie
always brought more.

SMILEY PENROD

I had good pie every yr for I don't know how long.
Smiley Penrod got my pie. I don't know if it was
accidental or some one told him it was mine but we
had to eat with whoever bought. I sure wasn't happy
about it.

MAX JONES

We would have the Program or ~~sifer~~ chyper. I didn't want to do one and the teacher said you won't have to. Just say you didn't want too. But when it came time, some one choose me. I said no but the teacher said that wouldn't look nice for the School. Just go on. It was against Max Jones and he just started to High School. I just knew he would beat me but do you know I beat him. That made me feel pretty good.

ROSCOE HANEY

The only man teacher I had was a Sub. for Helen Wilson. His name was Roscoe Haney.

GRADUATION

When I took the 7th Grade exams I had to go to Troy. I
rode a horse over to Troy took the exams and rode all
the way back. It was quite a deal for me. I passed the
test alright. That was when we lived in the Log Cabin
and went to Oak Hill School.

◀ Vetra, left, and sister Reva Padget, appear ready for a trip to town, circa 1930. Courtesy of Leon Wilkinson.

COUNTRY DANCES

We had country dances first one house then another. They would remove the furniture. Dance all nite. We always had a big crowd. We hardly ever got home before daylight. Paul and I done the shodish. No one else did this dance but once or twice an evening they all yelled for us to dance. Most every time they would throw nickels, dimes and quarters on the floor for us. We done pretty good for those times. I don't remember where we learned it.

DANCE ALL NIGHT

When we had these dances the kids danced every
dance all nite. Boy we had a time. In the winter if we
had snow we took the horses and went on the sled.
Kinda cold but went any way.

THE LONG WAY HOME

We went to Bill Petits for a dance once. They had 17 or 18 kids and lived South of Troy. Well we started home a bit early and Dad was lit to the gills. Well he didn't turn one corner and run in the ditch. Turned the car over. We all got out. No one got hurt. There we all were no way to get home couldn't get the car out. Well George Cruikshank he was drunker than Dad but he offered to take us home. We got in his car. Mom wouldn't let him drive faster than 5 mi an hr. Hardly moving. When we got to Bill and Effie Barkers first house South of Oak Hill School Mom had him stop and we stayed there. George went back and helped Dad and Clell get the car out. We had a Model T and the top was wore out so we drove it without the top.

ELDON FAIR

Dad used to get season tickets for the Eldon fair. We save our pennys for the fair. Some times we went every day at the fair. We had a lot of fun us kids did. Spent our money we saved. If we didn't have any money we would run around and look at things and watch the horse races. A big deal. Some times we would pull weeds for the neighbors and save our money for the fair.

NO ONE ELSE WENT THAT WAY

I remember Mom wouldnt let us go barefooted.
We must have our legs covered. If we didn't have
any shoes she would buy us a pr of long black
stockings we had to wear without shoes. It was
embarresing. No one else went that way.

TENT SHOW

Us kids had lots of fun we thot. They had a show
tent. Toby and Suze and their troope was the
players. Before the show they sold boxes of candy.
If you got the lucky ticket in the candy you got
a prize. I won a few times. They also had a tent
where you could throw balls and try to knock
the dolls down. And a few other games. Once in a
while Toby and Suze gave us a little bit of money
for helping pick up papers and boxes in the tent.

SOURCES

Acts and Joint Resolutions Passed at the Regular Session of the Forty-first General Assembly of the State of Iowa, State of Iowa: 1925 (pp. 39–45). http://books.google.com.

American Photographers of the Depression. Introduction by Charles Hagen. New York: Pantheon Books, 1985.

"Annual Fox Chase at Floris a Great Success." *The Iowa Homestead* 7 Oct. 1920: 28. http://www.crpubliclibrary.newspaperarchive.com.

Clark, Dan Elbert, "Recent Liquor Legislation in Iowa," *Iowa Journal of History and Politics, Volume 15,* State Historical Society of Iowa: 1917 (pp. 42–70). http://books.google.com.

Covert, Dennis. Personal interviews. 14 Oct. 2012, 10 Nov. 2012.

Covert, Floyd. Personal interviews. 25 Aug. 2012, 9 Sept. 2012, 11 Nov. 2012.

Covert, William. Personal interviews. 9 Sept. 2012, 11 Nov. 2012.

Durham, Betty. Personal interviews. 2011–2012.

Fifteenth Census of the United States, 1930, Salt Creek Township, Davis County, Iowa, Roll 651, Page 4B, Enumeration District 15, Image 787.0. http://www.ancestry.com.

Fourteenth Census of the United States, 1920, Union Township, Davis County, Iowa, Roll T625_485, Page 1A, Enumeration District 14, Image 1069. http://www.ancestry.com.

Guthrie, Sheri. Personal interview. 12 Oct. 2012.

Harding, Alvie, and Mable Harding. *The Ghost Mining Town of Laddsdale, Iowa, 1872–1918*. Ottumwa: Ottumwa Printing, 1971.

Machen, Lewis H., "Recent Temperance Legislation in Iowa," *Extracts from Liquor Laws of Prohibition States*, Virginia Legislative Reference Bureau: 1916 (pp. 69–79). http://books.google.com.

Padget, Donald. Personal interviews. 9 Sept. 2012, 20 Nov. 2012.

Plat Book of Davis County, Iowa. Rockford: W. W. Hixson & Co., 1930. http://digital.lib.uiowa.edu/u?/hixson,1876. Online image from the University of Iowa Libraries/Iowa Digital Library. Original image in the University of Iowa Libraries Map Collection.

"Report of Board of Parole," *Legislative Documents Submitted to the General Assembly of the State of Iowa, Volume V*, State of Iowa: 1919 (pp. 8–55). http://books.google.com.

The New 11 x 14 Atlas of the World. Chicago: Rand McNally & Co., Engravers, 1895. http://www.livgenmi.com/1895/IA/state.htm. Digitized image modified and reproduced with permission. Copyright © 2011 by www .MemorialLibrary.com.

Wilkinson, Leon. Personal interviews. 25 June 2012, 20 Nov. 2012.